Anne has spent her entire career serving her community as a registered nurse and family nurse practitioner. She is currently working full-time as a nurse practitioner in the field of intellectual and developmental disabilities. She also has formed her own PLLC, where she serves clients in the community focusing on mental, spiritual and physical wellness. She has published various nursing articles related to the practice of developmental disabilities care and support, has presented at various local and national conferences on topics related to ID/DD over the past two decades to nurses from all over the country. She is the mother of five children, and grandmother to four. In her spare time, she loves hiking, cooking, baking, camping, traveling, reading and kayaking, as well as spending time with her horses.

ANNE CAMPBELL

YOU ARE
MY PERSON

AUSTIN MACAULEY PUBLISHERS®

LONDON * CAMBRIDGE * NEW YORK * SHARJAH

Ordering Information
Quantity sales: Special discounts are available on quantity purchases by corporations, associations, and others. For details, contact the publisher at the address below.

Publisher's Cataloging-in-Publication data
Campbell, Anne
YOU ARE MY PERSON

ISBN 9798895434079 (Paperback)
ISBN 9798895434086 (Hardback)
ISBN 9798895434093 (e-pub e-book)

Library of Congress Control Number: 2024926408

www.austinmacauley.com/us

First Published 2025
Austin Macauley Publishers LLC
40 Wall Street
33rd Floor, Suite 3302
New York, NY 10005 USA

mail-usa@austinmacauley.com
+1 (646) 5125767

To Keygen, my person, for the joy and peace you have given me, and for inspiring me daily to be the very best that I can be.

All of my love, forever and always,

Your Person (aka Grandma)

No words could ever express how thankful I am for the endless support of my village, each of you have stood with and behind me on this crazy adventure, for without you, I would have been lost. You know who you are. It truly does take a village to raise a family and I am so blessed to have you.

To Ron and his wonderful wife Kristin… thank you for being my rock and my safety, guiding me every step of the way on this journey.

To Bobette, thank you for tagging along on our adventures, the Impromptu coffee deliveries (sometimes with bourbon), and the endless support and encouragement, as well as 'tough love' when needed…

I would like to give special thanks to my mom, Dennis, and children for all of the help, love encouragement along the way. There are no words to thank you enough.

To my very best friend Paulette, it is my sincerest hope that this fledgling work provides you and Liam with the tribute you also so desperately deserve and gives you hope… as we are kindred spirits in this adventure. All of my love to you and Liam.

I am your person, and you are mine,
when it rains and when it shines.

You came to me on a cold winter day,
I took you into my arms, and I knew you'd stay.

You are my person, and I am yours,
your tiny feet wake me as they run over the floor.

You come down the hallway and peek through the
door, climb into my bed to snuggle some more.

I am your person, and you are mine,
you love to run and love to climb.

I take you fishing, and we walk to the creek,
I hold your hand to keep you on your feet.

You are my person, and I am yours,
I watch you sleep and hear you snore.

We read books together and I rock you to sleep,
take walks in the forest and pick rocks to keep.

I am your person, and you are mine,
you love to help bake, especially pies.

We read the recipe and roll out the dough,
you sneeze as you send flour blowing like snow.

You are my person, and I am yours,
I walk you to school and give hugs at the door.

I whisper, "Love you buddy", and you whisper back,
"I love you more!"

I am your person, and you are mine,
we gaze at the stars and the moon, as they shine.

We sit on a blanket and watch the sea,
look for cool shells, and fly kites in the breeze.

You are my person, and I am yours, we walk through the mountains, and watch eagles soar.

We play with your puppy and give him treats and laugh while he tickles your toes and your feet.

I am your person, and you are mine,
when you are scared, and you want to hide.

I say, "Go away monsters" and spray "monster spray"
Check your room and your closet to keep them away.

I am always with you and forever will be,
I was sent to you, and you were sent to me.

I hold you close and smooth your hair,
I give you squeezes to show you I care.

Throughout space and forever in time,
I will be yours and you will be mine.

No matter what happens, and whatever we do,
you belong to me, and I belong to you.

THE END